Among the Fierce Eves
Gayle Elen Harvey

For Nellie, Dorothea, Laura D., Jenny M., Helene W.,
Bennett and Spike--- who gave me the gift, so long ago,
of believing in poetry as a way of life---

Among the Fierce Eves
©2009, Gayle Elen Harvey
ISBN 13: 978-1-934828-04-5

Spire Press, 532 LaGuardia Pl, Ste 298, New York, NY 10012
www.spirepress.org

Acknowledgements

The author wishes to thank the following publications in which these poems, or versions of them, first appeared:

Ekphrasis, Heart: A Journal of Spiritual Writing, Nomad's Choir, Lalimbata and Panhandler-----

"It's Raining in Arles"--- Kimera---1st prize

Among the Fierce Eves
Contents

Badia Alterpiece

("The Annunciation"---panel---Lorenzo Monaco 1410-15)

Independent of this story, no mere
figment,
they encounter each other among madder blue cascades, vermilion
patternings
of their garments.
Nothing is clearer than the Virgin's essential self,
her invisible music like snow without
the coldness.
But her cobalt cloak anchors her, this young girl without grand gestures,
knowing only the real
world.

Gabriel, in contrast, is a ritual
of conviction,
his tunic flowing backwards into echoes of jasper.
Released from vigilance, he brings her a future that is pure,
that's authentic, that is already
underway.

Nothing's accidental, a burn
of shyness
welling-up inside both of them.
She has not been asked, yet, to disrobe, reveal her modesty,
but, willingly submits to those whispers
of flesh, until she's carried to the unforeseeable,
till she is purely
born.

Magdalene at the Cross

(after Guttisa's " "Crucifixion"-------)

Sundered
in the raucous air, barely inches
above her, His body's gouged spectacle shudders into that space
He must pass through without
her.

Time stops
with betrayal, a slumping of shoulders, His shadow wrapped
taut, gray winding-sheet
of sorrow.
She cannot grasp this, something
over with.

Naked,
she remembers their last night together, in a garden's green
exuberance
just before He was taken, without a backward
glance.

For the savor
of sin, she was never That Woman.
Without His mouth
to her rapture, what became of such rumor's, pedestrian
jealousies?

All around her,
crowds gamble and brawl as He disappears in a surging
of bloodlust and vinegar, a silence that's "alpha
and omega".

What
has He given, how much of her has He
taken?
Hope, the denial of it for 3 days until dawn's holy
transformation.

 "Do not touch me."

His immaculate
weight, her recovery, with desire, only subtext, the years ahead,
over which may come healing.
Filled with grace, she continues to say it,
His Name.

"The Ecstasy of St. Theresa"

(Bernini-----Cornara Chapel--------------)

Oh, she's in ecstasy alright, eternal embrace
of gilt and candle-lit marble,
head tossed back, those saintly eyes, half-closed, her mouth,
wide-open.

And you stare, you cannot look
away, her presence more
than visceral,
her soul, raw, inflicted.
Is it love of God that's swept her breast, that's taken her
to lie in the clutch of this jeweled wood
and incense.

Or is it lust that abrades imagination,
that lifts her
to such voracious heights, she risked the brink
of carnal blasphemy.

For now, she is motionless, her soul
relinquished,
acknowledged offering,
one more permanent, celestial
wound.

Winter Advisory

Still waiting for better news, storm shadows
advance,
skating overhead.
Interludes of silence before winds scowl,
still mildly.

The air's haunted at the edges with chill
tremors.
Hooks of light turn the solid sky white
and howling
through the oncoming
snows.

This Decade's Harsh Beginning

never mind that on the Leader's desk, *Reader's Digest*
and a collection of *Nehi* bottle-caps. Devastation

is shadowing every voting booth.
The full moon, having just lost her virginity,

confesses that she's the niece of a German reformer.
Every widow in Georgetown votes Republican,

their daughters and sons are Marines killed
in the Green Zone.

One widow, a poet, can't bring herself to leave
the spot-light. On the podium,

her latest book, Holy Ruthlessness,
(It's Human Nature to Survive.)

Procedural Notes for Nation Building

Amid wars
and their levelings,
into what sorry distance the easily damaged
are ruddled and slagged, startled up by the predator's
wing beat.

Poor prisoners of shock and
awe,
death claims the whole orbit
with global politics.

The veiled face will not forget you.

How much secrecy is too much before the fates devour
everything
but on a need to know basis.

Shot at close range,
who's to blame for what's happening---

Fallen blossoms lit deep,
neither this night
not the next, stops the terrible weeping.
The veiled face
wont forget you---

Let it end
Now.

"They Are Walking In Bare Feet Over Violence------- "
(Brent Armendinger------------------------)

With only banishment
for an offering,
they robe themselves in mute saffrons
like a harvest moon
before its final hours, before its sudden
departure.

Teargas empties the neighborhood.
In any country,
on every continent, repression is never
reticent.
Now and forever,
it does what it does, its wreckage
lessens us.

Too late for the safety of higher ground,
they move ahead willingly,
with deference,
down the endless road.
They clutch their chests, stumble, they are
rounded up.

It happens.

Waving torn flags
of indifference, rip their tongues
loose
into silence, this indifferent
calm.

(for the Monks of Burma---)

North of Here

("Divers find sunken bus with 49 drowned.
   The group, many handicapped, was returning from a
   French comedy---") AP news item

The highway hums, accelerates, its burden breaking, now,
in small pieces, telling
no one
the bus is missing
from rear-view mirrors.

There is nothing
for awhile.

The lake's a well-kept secret. No one knows how much
the children laughed, who spoke
about the warm mugs
of cocoa,
mothers waiting with cookies
at a small, kitchen table.

Nothing

breaks the tender mouth
of darkness.
North of here, a father's rubbing sleep
from worried eyes.
Crutches drift, impartial fish.
Coats and shoes wake,
empty,

North of here, the moon floats, sweater-less,
a dead weight.

Katrina, First Anniversary

Under layers of devastation, all things concrete
and metal, unforgiving---
Made and broken, not yet put back together,
the kind of silence beyond memory,
more intense than the storm, itself, having risen
to the heights of a city, its stench
amid ruin, every sprout
of mold.

What of those who predicted how the elements
would, one day,
line up?

The Dead ghost every missing room.
Tolling
among the fierce eaves,
groaning elegies
enfold
the drowned.

Left Among Losses

Looking the other way, erratic hugs
inescapable,
you are stung and small
at the same time,
an empty
circle, a blank
wall.

Night asps darken
like urns
while the moon weeps from great distances,
a lute without
strings.

Here, in the kneeling, inside these black
depths,
grief can never work
as it was meant
to.

"It's Raining In Arles"

(Marjorie Agosin-----)

Winds rarely touch
down--- those few stars remaining, continue whirling
on their soused stems.
Between mistral and accord, there are very few secrets.
His church, now, is desolate
and guttural.

He's an olive tree lost in its own pensive
emptiness.
This orchard is not his home
or the garden.

There are no purple irises.

What is real? What's imagined--- Crows are wearing
his shadow and it moves and it flaps its wings.
And it soars and it
ends.

There's no comfort, no mistaking the abyss,
its known sanctum.

Wheat-fields shatter his aura
with thc ricochet
of voices.
Their nattering.

Arrival escapes him.
Rain swallows him up, its umbra, its smother
in the yellow house
of his soul.

Elegy, December

(for Agha Shahid Ali, in memory---------)

Kashmiri still pollen
on the lips,
your breathing disconnects. Not a
whisper.
It is one day past sunset when the news comes
to break us.

Infinity stalked you
like a saffron-eyed tiger.
Beloved,
as the reed flute is torn from Jhelum's riverbank,
too soon,
was your soul snatched from the body's
commitment.
Its final rehearsal.

Bereaved, we weep
in the curve of your dimming reflection.
Mourning you,
we travel from poem to poem, the moon gone
before us.

Gates open. You hover,
an eloquence among ankle bells
and oil lamps, ululations
of lilies.
Your words breach the dark---they moisten our tongues
like clear water.

Stars peck at a heavier
horizon.
"As-salamu--- Alaykum"
White-veiled, the Himalayas shift silently.
Night begins lying down
among its blue
stones.

Charles River, Sunset

Of the late October sun, so volatile, lush, only tatters
remain, a few drops
of blood,
though the skyline's slow to lose
its ravishing color.

In the distance, Cambridge nestles
and burns.
Joggers swarm the mallow overpass as we move easily
from tree to tree.

The hour turns ominous, the moon's backing away,
clinking delicate pieces of silver.
Thick-bellied, sly,
it could swallow us whole.

This is the way of the world, damage free-lance,
in spite of the river's shuddering with
lit spires,
summer's fever.

Our lips gleam with the tart juice
of deception.
Love, the water disappears and the skies,
concealing a squadron of lusts,
are awash
with your going.

After 8 Years, We Leave Together, Missing Each Other
(for Jules-----------)

Only hours apart, our scheduled flights called,
we're drawn upward, leveling
at last---
The planes blip, disappear from Logan's radar, carry us
toward separate lives, that awkward clip
of other languages.

Another post-card and I think of you, your face like April
dimming in those mirrored
verticals,
that varied Boston sky-line, lush
with its full moon.

Blossom among blossoms, spring might easily beguile us,
over-ride desire---
I can't phone you, so describe magnolias scalloping
a cobbled avenue,
the cadmium forsythia, azaleas' warning lights---
"Adapt. Survive."

Ambivalent, less traveled, I rise above death's salt flats,
falling back, again,
to no-man's land, the sanctuary
of my own backyard.

I must offer less than chill lips which have lied,
repeatedly, to keep you
at a distance---
I can't ask how many years must pass
before we see each other, naked and exposed, once more
by chance,
come this close.

For The Man Who Signed At Mary Oliver's Reading

Fluid in the evening air, his arms lift her poems,
an easy transcendence
like egret wings, his fingers, a keyboard,
accomplice
to her rounding words.

Her pages float upward.

He contours, fluently, a poem's baseline,
its value.
He opens each of them, the smell of marsh reeds
grief's upheaval
sweeping over the audience.
Fists tremble, explain that hidden light
in each stanza.

His signing's a sacrament, an aria, a duet
of engagement.

Hands flutter, they punctuate, they whisper
like the gills of a speckled trout
in a black pond,
the April moon lucent in this silence
of listening.

"The Turtle-Sighing Tree"

(Rebecca Horn---1994-----------)

Eons are swallowed
whole.
Reptilian, barely cognitive, but weighty
with evolution,
you struggle from the water's depths, from tugging
mud-tides.
Earth is revisioned as you struggle through figments
of ocean.

Bound from solitude
and marsh grass, through salt hay, this landscape,
awash, now, with audibles the color
of pollens and willow.

An aged-metal moon surges
genderless
beneath a smelter of stars, their solder and weld,
enigmas
of solar clatter.

Dense with all this cold,
you re-enter the cusped sea, its thrall
of dark plunder, this undoing
that heals.

"Buddha's Court"

(Helen Frankenthaler-----1964)

Out of chaos
and its chafing snows,
comes a kind of bliss that's unlanguaged,
more than intimate, a perfect timbre
of colors.

Out of hunger,
its sudden clarity,
you wake to nurturing, its colors startling
as orchids.

Silence.
Its total focus, its codas
of color begin edging toward
the center.

You're enveloped
in tuber roses.
Their colors, curious, a place of shy syllables,
a perfect circle,
a hallowed realm just the width
of your hand.

"The Phenomenon of Ecstasy"

(Salvadore Dali---1933----------------)

Begins as an aria, tight-fisted as lust
rung
almost stunningly, noticed
barely
in the beginning
until opened-up brings that silence
of a coral gate
turned
transparent.

The spine thaws, desire
flourishes,
its text besmirched with spilled
honey.

Breasts burgeon, the hips more pliant
than lilies.

Flesh becomes another nearing
star
without plot-lines, its chimes
inaudible
more than deeply, more than light-years,
exploitations
of joy.